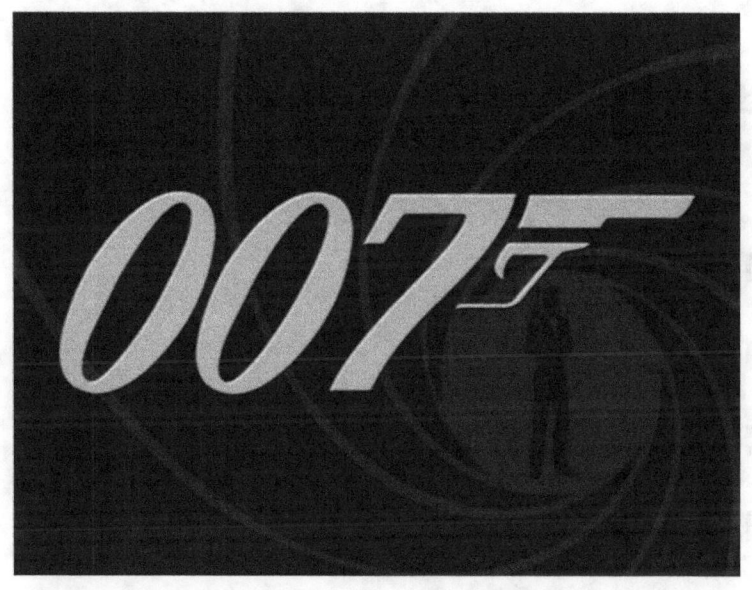

# The James Bond 007 Effect:

# An analysis of the mega-movie hit, James Bond 007

# The James Bond 007 Effect:

## An analysis of the mega-movie series, James Bond 007

### *Contents*

# 1. Introduction

Never has a series of movies had such an effect on the global film audience than James Bond 007. If one was to ask our parents and grandparents their favourite movie, *James Bond 007* would feature somewhere there, if not are number one. Other movies have come and gone, but this series of action/drama movies are legendary and will live on forever, as long as film exists. Just ask a man who would they like to be, and the answer could well come back as *James Bond 007*. But it was the actors and actresses who made up the films that made it all the more appealing and memorable, such as Sean Connery and Roger Moore and Money Penny. There would definitely be arguments over which era of *James Bond 007* movies was the best, the Sean Connery-Roger Moore era or from Pierce Brosnan onwards. Most older generations prefer the previous era while the younger generations like the latter eras. However, the previous eras have had the most affect on viewers and fans.

Current movie makers of the contemporary Bond era have tried to reproduce the magic of Bonds from yesteryear. Something was salvaged, in the sense of the action, but older generations can see the difference with the story, dialogue, style and suave all needing some help. Then again, some prefer the older Bonds and that's it. They were so used to the previous Bonds that nothing, no matter who they are, compares. But this could possibly change with the modern James Bonds gradually getting better. Another quality of the *James Bond 007* movies was the original creator, author, producer and director *Ian Fleming*. Fleming had a way about him and he put this into the *James Bond 007* collection. Some, if not most, would say he was the original and the best, so let's see who can match it with Fleming, such as Jeremy Dunns, Barry Eisler, Gayle Lunds and Brett Battles (Los Angeles Times (November 10, 2012)).

## 2. Subjects

**The Movie**

Never has a movie been watched so often as in James Bond (Box Office Mojo ). People can watch the series of films over and over, from television to DVD, and still enjoy them. This movie has it all, with action, drama, style and fashion, technology, love and passion, cinematography, music, good and evil, dialogue, occasional humour and a strong story theme. The movies earned a considerable amount of revenue when they were at the box office. However, the recent instalment in the modern era has seen Skyfall with Daniel Craig surpass Thunderball at the box office and become one of the all-time successful movies worldwide. According to Box Office Mojo, all of Daniel Craig's films have had the most successful response at the box office. Pierce Brosnan's films were popular, following Daniel Craig, and then came the previous James Bond era with *Golden Eye* and *Moonraker* (Box Office Mojo). Perhaps people were not used to or had heard of *James Bond 007* back then compared to now.

People are more used to James Bond these days and want to see a different or unique approach with the new movies. In stating this, the old James Bonds are legendary and will live on forever and have a similar affect today like when they were first viewed all those years back. *Arnold Schwarzenegger* movies have been another successful action film franchise in contemporary society with movies like *Terminator 1 & 2*, *Total Recall* and *Predator*. A number of popular and successful action stars have surfaced since the old James Bond films, like Schwarzenegger, and others like *Sylvestor Stallone* and *Bruce Willis*. But James Bond would have definitely influenced these actors and actresses to become action stars. Additionally, similar Bond-like films have been made with *The Bourne Ultimatum* with

*Matt Damon* and popular comedies with *Mike Myers' Austin Powers* (Personal Experiences – Watched various action movies/Personal Experiences- University).

As stated before, the Bond films have a good mix of themes that make it so unique. Somehow *Ian Fleming* and current Bond movie makers seem to make it flow together well, although the old Bond films would have to win. It is difficult to mention what exactly makes the Bond movies so good as all the themes and elements work off each other. To narrow it down, the cinematography was most probably a central feature, as was the style and suave and dialogue. There could have been other actors selected to pick James Bond, but these actors were chosen, such as George Lazenby, Sean Connery, Roger Moore, Timothy Dalton, Pierce Brosnan and Daniel Craig.

Of course these Bond figures did a fantastic job, as shown by the quality, success and popularity of the films. Sean Connery would probably have to be the most popular James Bond. Connery was a normal person like everybody else, aiming to make it big in acting. When Connery was chosen and acted in James Bond, it was obvious to see, with the help of genius movie maker Ian Fleming, this actor had something to offer (Personal Experiences – Watched James Bond 007 movies/ Personal Experiences- University).

The Sean Connery-Roger Moore eras were around the time when colour had first been introduced to film. The colour looked unbelievable, but this was not enough. The cinematography in Bond was exceptional, thanks to the movie makers and the actors and actresses. Some movies in contemporary society are disjointed, too fast, too slow or all over the place, but James Bond 007 just flowed. The movie clips and cinematography had crispness and clarity, and were clean and good. Bond was one of the first movies of its kind, so it was important to make the effort to make it good. The settings and locations were also a feature and important, creating the perfect stage for the films. They showed Bond, as he would do as a secret agent, travelling around the world, and there were some great footage of the different settings and locations, from France to Italy to Africa. All the actors and actresses, as well as extras in the movie, all worked together perfectly to create the Bond scenes (Personal Experiences – Watched James Bond 007 movies/ Personal Experiences- University).

## Themes

## Themes – Good and Evil

The main theme of each Bond film is the battle between good and evil. It almost seems impossible for one man, in *James Bond 007*, to take on such a juggernaut of evil power by himself, as shown in the Bond films. But somehow, this Superman-like figure seems to pull it off. The evil side have all the money, all the technology, all the power. But Bond working **as a secret agent** for the British government, would have made him powerful and very intimidating to the evil powers that be, especially because he works on the side of the law and justice.

It is amazing to see a lone figure in Bond make his way into the mere centre of the evil side's headquarters and wreak havoc. Perhaps evil wants to keep on the good side of the law and let Bond in, for they know that if they kill someone from the law and British government, they would eventually get caught and be in trouble. But the evil side's power, in their minds, would give them permission to surpass or override this (Personal Experiences – Watched James Bond 007 movies/ Personal Experiences- University).

## Themes – Style, Suave and Power

There is even a web-site dedicated to Bond in a Google search under *James Bond 007* called 'Bond Lifestyle' and has all the style and suave that was Bond ([Bond Lifestyle](#)). This is a big area for the influence of James Bond on the public. People were mimicking what Bond and the Bond cast would wear, their hair, cologne, their drink and food (Martini, shaken not stirred), the cars and their gadgets, like watches. Bond always looked well groomed and yet somehow managed to not even raise a hair when taking on the bad guys. The technology was not mentioned on the Bond Lifestyle web-site as this was too high-tech for the general public, especially Bond's toys of weaponry for his enemies.

Could you imagine a member of the general public, untrained and uncontrolled, gaining access to this sort of weaponry? Yet, there are places in the world where people can gain access to weapons more easily than normal, for example, America. It would be a disaster. Although, having members of the general population, and of course Bond fans, try out these gadgets or weaponry under supervision would be an option, like hiring out a sports car such as a Ferrari. A business or group should start up an initiative called The Bond Experience, almost like The Amazing Race and Survivor, or businesses have Bond-like products and services to cater to Bond fans (Personal Experiences – Watched James Bond 007 movies/ Personal Experiences- University).

## Themes – Love and Passion

The love and passion in *James Bond 007* was almost out of a *Mills and Boon novel*. It was over-the-top and extravagant, but full of life and vitality, similar to a soapie on television like *Days of our Lives*, *Bold and the Beautiful* and *Young and the Restless*. Of course, it is usually the females watching these types of shows, but it is good to include the men in on these shows from time-to-time. You would never see Bond being passive or submissive, begging for some love and affection. Instead, Bond was very much the dominant figure in the situation and scenes, the rescuer and Cupid, and would usually get things started in love scenes – 'Oh James'.

The Bond girls come from a variety of backgrounds, almost like the settings and locations that Bond was filmed in, and of course each had a beauty unique to them. It was great to see movie makers respecting the different nationalities in the Bond movies and not just staying with British girls, since Bond was a British agent. But then again, it was like love-on-the-run and was indicative of the life of a secret agent, not real life for the rest of the population, creating a form of escapism and indulgence. This would have been mixed emotions for people who would have liked to have had the love and passion that Bond created in a more normal situation (Personal Experiences – Watched James Bond 007 movies/ Personal Experiences- University).

## Themes – Dialogue and Communication

Another element of James Bond that people admired and liked to copy was the dialogue and communication in the movies. An example of this was the talk between Bond and the Bond girls, including Miss Moneypenny, and Bond's conversations with the bad side. Style and suave came into play here, as mentioned previously, as did charm and grace, with Bond as the dominant male figure, most probably an Omega character for his clothing choices, words and conversation, style and charisma. There were known and expected lines that came from Bond, taking in some exceptions in line with the movie theme and plot, for example, 'Bond, James Bond'.

Bond was direct, smooth and silky with what he said and how he said it. Some, if not most of the dialogue would have been gained from Ian Fleming and his novels and the initial script for the movie. It would have been interesting if the Bond actors came up with some of their own lines to add to and spice up the script of the movie. Ian Fleming was different and exceptional, his thinking was that of someone who thought outside-the-square, original and creative, and this came through in the dialogue of the Bond films. Fleming would definitely be one of the originators of action and crime novels, which we see a plethora of today. The dialogue, combined with other elements of the Bond movies, made for exciting movie watching (Personal Experiences – Watched James Bond 007 movies/ Personal Experiences- University).

## The Characters

There were some common and central characters in the Bond films. First obviously there was James Bond 007, then the Bond girl, Miss MoneyPenny Lois Maxwell, Q or Quartermaster for the gadgets, head of MI6, the boss of the criminal syndicate and the boss' main stand-over man and woman.

## James Bond 007

With regards to Bond, it would be quite a risk, if not detrimental to change the way he did things. For example, his greeting to Money Penny, how he has his Martini shaken not stirred, his famous line - 'Bond, James Bond'. Bond will always be Bond, obviously with different actors playing Bond, but it would be his reaction to people, events and situations that shows his variant personality and character and skills. It would have been more of a task for the new Bonds to match and re-create the magic of the previous Bond eras, but this was achieved to some extent, especially with the success of these new Bond movies at the box office.

It was great to see some variety in the actors playing Bond and this would have appealed to different groups. It would have been interesting if movie makers stayed with the one Bond throughout, which they did for certain periods with Connery, Moore, Brosnan and Craig (007James, Characters, 'James Bond 007'/ Personal Experiences – Watched James Bond 007 movies/ Personal Experiences- University).

Bond had to deal with a lot of things all happening at the same time in his role. He was firstly and most importantly a secret agent, which dictated most, if not all of what he did. This job as a secret agent was tedious, detailed and dangerous. Bond makes it look effortless, but a real-life secret agent would have had a tougher task, particularly staying alive. Then again, a master and professional in their chosen field would also have this grace and power, almost like singing the gospel song Amazing Grace. Bond managed to fit in his various Bond girls during his role as a secret agent, who provided great company for him during this time.

But Bond most probably wanted the Bond girls on the surface but needed them deep down to help, support and love him and confirm his male dominance. It was amazing Bond was titled 007. Perhaps 001 would have been a better choice as he was always the man, or secret agent, chosen by MI6' to get the job done. Maybe the numerals 007 meant he was good but had some rough edges, or made a bit of a mess where he went and therefore the other agents probably got the job done cleaner and quieter (007James, Characters, 'James Bond 007'/ Personal Experiences – Watched James Bond 007 movies/ Personal Experiences- University).

## Bond Girls

The Bond girls provided that extra 'oomph' that Bond needed to do his job as a secret agent. It was almost like a husband and wife role in some sort of crazy way. Bond would have been the money-earner as a secret agent and the Bond girl at home waiting for him with love and passion. It would have been an interesting scenario if Bond had a true wife at home, who knew or did not know he was a secret agent. One would definitely be correct in stating if Bond needed the girl with him, especially at the best of times, like when caught in the bad side's lair. It was like he had to save himself as well as the Bond girl, making it all the more effort.

But somehow Bond still managed it, making it look effortless. But some of these Bond girls could handle themselves, knowing how to talk and carry out hand-to-hand combat. It was like the modern era of husband and wife where both are working, or like an own-business where Bond runs the business and the Bond girl, his wife, is his secretary. It was different if the Bond girl was a secret agent as well, but sometimes they were not. Bond also manages to fit in some love and affection, even whilst in the criminals' company, almost like a dying wish in the criminal's eyes.

The girls in Bond reinforce his role as the dominant Alpha-Omega male, and are almost like his sidekick in the movie (007James, Characters, 'List of All James Bond Girls'/ Personal Experiences – Watched James Bond 007 movies/ Personal Experiences- University). Ursula Andress, as Honey Ryder, from *Dr. No* in 1952 was voted the most popular Bond girl. She had looks, a meek voice, was tough yet humble, and of course stuck by Sean Connery's side as James Bond. Some Bond girls dressed in Bikinis whilst others were more conservative. Sometimes Bond's charm and power was so influential he managed to change the bad girl to good, making her a good Bond girl, for example, Domino Derval in *Thunderball* and Jill Masterton in *Goldfinger*. Some of the names of the Bond girls were sexually orientated, such as Pussy Galore and Plenty O'Toole, and would have been funny and entertaining and arousing on one hand, but also rude and crude for older generations of Bond (007James, Characters, 'List of All James Bond Girls'/ Personal Experiences – Watched James Bond 007 movies/ Personal Experiences- University)

## Miss MoneyPenny

Miss Moneypenny, originally Lois Maxwell, was almost like the hidden Bond girl of James Bond. Money Penny was good-looking but had charm and dressed and acted conservatively, obviously as MI6s' secretary. She was an opposite to the Bond girls Bond was used to. She resembled the dedicated and faithful housewife Bond could come home to, as if she was maintaining his work-home office. It is questionable whether it had entered Bond's mind if he had considered Money Penny as someone he would go out with or even marry.

Bond's 'hi-and-bye' routine, mixed in with some light flirting and affection, confirmed Bond's charm and diplomacy, but also that it was still a business relationship. Those wishes from Money Penny could have helped Bond in a number of ways, even without him possibly knowing it. MoneyPenny though, for that short space and time, also confirmed Bond's male dominance, like the other Bond girls (007James, Characters, 'Miss Moneypenny'/ Personal Experiences – Watched James Bond 007 movies/ Personal Experiences- University).

## Q or Quartermaster

Desmond Llewelyn played Q (Quartermaster) in 17 James Bond films. Q was the gadget man for MI6 and would have been a good friend of Bond. It is a good choice to select an older man to play Q, such as Llewelyn, because he represents experience, knowledge and wisdom. Interesting enough, Q was also soft spoken, not intimidating for a gadget man towards Bond. Q had to be direct for a field like gadgets and weapons and had some dry humour, especially with his famous line - 'do be careful 007'. He was like Bond's indirect caring and cautious father-figure in the films. He made MI6's gadgets look easy-to-use and accessible.

Q may have contributed to the design and construction of these gadgets, not just a mouthpiece or spokesperson for them. MI6's gadgets could have come from the military or specially made by secret scientists, engineers and craftsmen. It is similar to Christian Bale as Batman and his father's top-level gadgets from his father's business empire, Wayne Enterprises. The only thing was that Bond was a secret agent and would have permission by the government and the law to use such gadgets, whereas Bruce Wayne had a big business behind him and big business, no matter how big and powerful they are, is not the government and the law. Batman lived above the law, whereas James Bond was the law (007James, Characters, 'Q'/ Personal Experiences – Watched James Bond 007 movies/ Personal Experiences- University).

## Head of M16

The head of MI6, looked relatively old in the older Bond films, like Q, but not as old. The head of M16 looked like an older wise and friendly confidante, business man or counsellor to Bond, other than being head of M16. He would only be seen for a short time in the Bond films, but showed mild authority, experience, knowledge and wisdom. A younger Ralph Fiennes plays the head of MI6 in the modern Bond, bringing energy and enthusiasm. He is also better looking than the previous head of MI6 in older Bond films, which would almost match in with Bond, being a younger-looking secret agent. This would surely allow him to understand and match in with Bond and his youthful looks and provide some competition for Bond who was also youthful and good looking.

The Bond movies show Bond always accepting his secret mission from the head of M16, which makes up the whole movie. It would be interesting to see a defiant Bond who does not accept a mission from the head of MI6, intending not to do it. As the saying goes, 'one step at a time', meaning Bond is only human and can only take on one mission at a time. The movie does not show Bond looking through the files and information as much, but seems to accept the mission blindly. This emphasises Bond's confidence and supposed strength in taking on his missions assigned to him by MI6 (007James, Characters, 'M'/ Personal Experiences – Watched James Bond 007 movies/ Personal Experiences- University).

## Head of Crime Syndicate

The boss of the crime syndicate that Bond had to deal with are often relaxed with a quiet confidence. It is always a he and would be quite a stir to have a female boss instead. They are usually rich and powerful and have enormous land ownership with their lairs possessing decorative surroundings, including big dining room tables, ornaments and technology, some of which Bond finds himself viewing and experiencing when confronting the boss. These criminal bases or headquarters look the way they do, all big and extravagant, for the sake of the movie.

The bosses in Bond are usually distinct characters, similar yet different to each other. They are well dressed, confident and have a number of perks as a sign of their riches and power, for example, gold for *Goldfinger*, space station for *Moonraker* and the white cat for *Octopussy*. The boss of MI6 is quite different to the boss of the criminal syndicate. The boss of MI6 is more refined, straight, direct and professional. The boss of the crime syndicate is decorative, defiant, sarcastic and ruthless.

However, the bosses of the crime syndicate seem to treat Bond well once he has made it into their base or headquarters. Perhaps this is a respect for the law since Bond is a British secret agent. A vigilante who is a good person would most probably not be treated so kindly by the crime syndicate. Yet the boss of the crime syndicate would attempt to do something to Bond and with Bond's expertise, skill and special gadgets, he always manages to get himself out of trouble (007James, Characters, 'Top 10 James Bond Villains'/ 'Auric Goldfinger'/ 'Dr. No'/ Personal Experiences – Watched James Bond 007 movies/ Personal Experiences- University).

## Crime Syndicate Stand-Over People

The head standover men and women in James Bond are more on Bond's level. The two standouts are Jaws, played by Richard Kiel, in *Moonraker*, and Robert 'Red' Shaw, the SPECTRE assassin in *From Russia With Love* (007James, Characters, 'Jaws'/ 'Red Grant'/ Personal Experiences – Watched James Bond 007 movies). Richard Kiel was the very tall and very strong man with the metal teeth, and Robert Shaw was the blonde haired, intelligent and brutish and strong assassin. It is great cinematography to see Bond and these head standover men and women do battle. Looks-wise, Bond seems clearly out of his class, but again, his expertise, skill and special gadgets come to the rescue, and of course he is the hero of the films. Bond even manages to change these bad criminal men and women to good at times, for example, Jaws falling in love with the diminutive, attractive blonde girl with glasses and the blonde haired stand over man shooting an offender who was going to shoot Bond when he was with the gypsies in *From Russia with Love*.

The boss of MI6 and Bond represent the good side while the boss of the crime syndicate and head standover man are from the bad side. The boss of the crime syndicate and head standover men seemed a bit more reserved and quieter compared to the boss of MI6 and Bond who seem more outspoken. Perhaps it was the bad side observing, listening and obeying to Bond to some extent, as shown in the movie when Bond confronts them. There is nothing spectacular about these criminal stand over men and women, but their looks are distinctive like their boss of the crime syndicate, for example Jaws and his metal teeth and the blonde Robert Shaw with his great strength and calm nature (007James, Characters, 'Top 10 James Bond Villains' / Personal Experiences – Watched James Bond 007 movies/ Personal Experiences- University).

## The Stars

Obviously James Bond was the central star of the series of Bond films. So it is only fitting to pay homage to the stars who played Bond, namely Sean Connery and Roger Moore and Pierce Brosnan and Daniel Craig. These stars will be focused on because they had the longest runs at playing *James Bond 007*.

## Sean Connery

As the most popular and successful Bond in the history of the Bond films, Sean Connery really did make a name for himself by playing James Bond 007. Connery was acting before he played the part of Bond. He held casual jobs to make ends meet and did acting as well. Bond would have provided fame and fortune for Connery and the rest of his life, even his family and descendants. Some might say, as with Roger Moore, if there was a need to act in other films after James Bond. The movies Connery acted in after Bond were great, for example, *The Rock*, *Highlander* and

*The League of Extraordinary Gentleman*, but not as good as Bond.

One would have to feel somewhat sorry for Connery because when someone thinks of Sean Connery, they think of *James Bond 007*. Nevertheless, Connery has acted in a large number of films before and after Bond, 74 in fact, which is very good by today's standards. Connery brought looks, that hunk-nature, style, charm, smoothness, debonair and that famous Scottish brogue to the Bond films, and also true grit, strategy, sarcasm and light humour with his other films. Connery could have also passed for Mediterranean in the Bond films, for example, Greek, Italian or Lebanese. Some viewers who were not accustomed to a Scottish brogue could have thought Connery was a foreigner from another country (Bio-graphy, 'Sean Connery biography'/ Personal Experiences – Watched James Bond 007 movies/ Personal Experiences- University

Connery won a number of acting awards, including an *Academy Award* and *Golden Globe*. He, like some others, has survived Hollywood, the acting scene and the world's knowledge about him, to live to a good old age. Hopefully he can live a bit longer. Connery would be good for movie making if he gave it a try. He has been in films long enough, and has had direct exposure to the genius of *Ian Fleming* and the Bond movie makers to have some idea of what should be in certain films.

If not a movie maker, Connery would make a great advisor and consultant and diplomat. He has that authoritative way about him with great communication skills and would serve a movie maker or related group or area well. The only thing is Connery is missing his Bond looks and youthfulness that many admired and loved him for and is appearing to be very much an old man, like a wise old sage. Of course Connery can still probably carry himself well and make those old looks become youthful, or a young man in an old man's body (Bio-graphy, 'Sean Connery biography'/ Personal Experiences – Watched James Bond 007 movies/ Personal Experiences- University).

**Roger Moore**

Roger Moore would definitely have to be close behind Sean Connery as one of the most popular and successful Bonds. Connery and Moore were the longest running Bonds. Moore had the advantage of playing similar roles to his part as *James Bond 007*. He played Simon Templar in the television series of The Saint and Lord Brett Sinclair in the adventure series of The Persuaders. The affect on Moore of playing *James Bond 007* was obvious, staying out of acting for five years before making a return. Moore's movies after Bond were not as spectacular after his role as Bond. In fact, many of the movies were not a success or heard much about compared to Connery's.

Moore acted in 59 films, less than Connery's. Moore was still set-up for life in the sense of fame and fortune, making his name in movie history as Bond. Yet he still had to walk around all the time with often being referred to as Bond. It would be interesting to hear how Moore, like Connery, had and has coped with this label of Bond (Bio-graphy, 'Roger Moore biography'/ Personal Experiences – Watched James Bond 007 movies/ Personal Experiences- University).

Moore, like Connery, has also lived to a good old age, getting through Hollywood. Obviously playing Bond called on certain elements in the role, like style and suave and charm, which Connery and Moore provided very well. Moore was cooler, calm and collected compared to Connery, who was louder, Alpha-Omegas male, and direct. Moore, as an English actor, had a straight accent compared to Connery who had a Scottish brogue and may have been harder to understand. Either way, Connery was Scottish and Moore was English, making them fitting for playing a British secret agent in Bond. Moore would have attracted a largely Anglo-Saxon audience with his English looks, as well as Bond and action movie lovers (Bio-graphy, 'Roger Moore biography'/ Personal Experiences – Watched James Bond 007 movies/ Personal Experiences- University).

Moore had the typical life of an actor. He was a model at an early age, did commercials for a few companies and acted in some B grade films before finally getting some attention with *The Saint* in 1962. Even being an actor did not stop Moore doing national service for the USA in the Royal Army Service Corps. To his credit he became a captain and commanded a small depot in West Germany.

Like many other actors, Moore went to an acting school, at the Royal Academy of Dramatic Art, were he also trained alongside the original Miss MoneyPenny, Lois Maxwell. *The Saint* and *James Bond 007* were Moore's longest films. *The Saint* would have provided vital training for playing the part of Bond, with Moore probably not even realising he was destined to play Bond, like Connery. His experience on The Saint was perhaps one of the reasons Moore was selected to play Bond, and of course Moore and Bond were a perfect fit (Bio-graphy, 'Roger Moore biography'/ Personal Experiences – Watched James Bond 007 movies / Personal Experiences- University).

## Pierce Brosnan

Pierce Brosnan could be said to be a cross between Connery and Moore looks wise. His Bond films were the first few Bond films in the new Bond era and tended to concentrate on the action side of things. Dialogue and story line were sacrificed for action with Bond using all the special gadgets and weaponry of

MI6 against his enemies. Of course, movie makers had to make the Brosnan-Bond films spectacular in a new era of Bond. Brosnan resembled Moore in a way, as compared to Connery, being a bit more plain and cool, calm and collected and soft-spoken. Some older viewers of Brosnan as *James Bond 007* tended to complain about this problem, stating how the films were one-sided and disjointed.

Brosnan looked a bit tired, unfit and out of his depth on a number of occasions, especially with face-to-face battles with bad guys. Brosnan tended to hide behind the special gadgets and weaponry that was *James Bond 007*. However, the action in the Brosnan-Bond films was first rate. Brosnan even got to be with some good-looking good and bad Bond females (Bio-graphy, 'Pierce Brosnan Biography'/ Personal Experiences – Watched James Bond 007 movies / Personal Experiences- University).

Pierce Brosnan is an Irish actor, which is almost like all of Great Britain, with Connery as Scottish and Moore as English. It is a coincidence how Brosnan's father is called Thomas, which is Connery's actual first name. Brosnan, like Moore, would have also attracted the Anglo-Saxon audiences, as well as Bond lovers and action-movie admirers. But his black locks, his hair, could have also had him as a mixture of nationality and therefore attracted other audiences. However, like Connery and Moore, Brosnan was from Great Britain but had a mixed accent, especially with his time in the USA. Those viewers who were from Great Britain would have, or could have picked his Irish accent, but maybe not other viewers.

Of the 59 films Brosnan has made, Brosnan had some good movies before and after Bond, similar to Connery, with *The Fourth Protocol, Mrs Doubtfire, Dante's Peak, The Matador, The Thomas Crown Affair, Mamma Mia and The Ghost Writer.* They even made Bond into a video game where Brosnan's voice was used (Bio-graphy, 'Pierce Brosnan Biography'/ Personal Experiences – Watched James Bond 007 movies; / Personal Experiences- University).

Like Moore, Brosnan went to drama school and was an environmentalist, also similar to Moore who gave to charity. As a young child, Brosnan's father abandoned his family as an infant and his mother moved to London to work as a nurse in London. Brosnan was therefore brought up by his extended family. Brosnan went from family member to family member, which would have left a mark on him. He was brought up a Roman Catholic in Ireland, but like some Irish Roman Catholics, has either lost his religion or found other means to keep the religion alive, with Brosnan believing in Buddhist philosophy. Brosnan however would still attend church from time-to-time where there is one available. Brosnan, like Moore, made brief appearances in films before making it in the American detective series, *Remington Steele*. Interestingly enough, like Moore in *The Saint*, Brosnan had a simllar role in *Remington Steele* and Bond movie makers would have most likely used this as selection for Brosnan to make it as Bond (Bio-graphy, 'Pierce Brosnan Biography'/ Personal Experiences – Watched James Bond 007 movies/ Personal Experiences- University).

**Daniel Craig**

Compared to Moore and Timothy Dalton, Daniel Craig had and showed a stronger physical nature about him, and also looked younger. He looked like Moore but more Arian and would have definitely attracted a larger Anglo-Saxon audience, possibly even more than Moore, Brosnan and Dalton. Craig was more straight and soft-spoken in his portrayal of Bond. Craig had some good dialogue in his Bond films, but lacked the charm and suave that Connery and Moore had. On Wikipedia, under Daniel Craig's profile, it is said Craig aimed at "bringing more 'emotional depth' to the Bond character", but Craig's expressions seem to show little emotion, apart from his many action scenes.

Unlike the other Bonds, Craig portrays a colder, almost meaner and ruthless Bond with his battles with the enemies, his love of women and when some die heartlessly in his job as a secret agent which was very different to Bond's time with the Bond girls in previous Bond films and his unquestionable acceptance of each mission from the head of MI6. However, Craig built on the good action of Dalton and Brosnan with more structured and theme-like action. His youthfulness and strong physical demeanour brought about some good action scenes (Biography, 'Daniel Craig Biography'/ Personal Experiences – Watched James Bond 007 movies/ Personal Experiences-University).

Craig is an English actor, like Moore, and also attended a drama school. Craig was early recognised through stage, like a Hugh Jackman-like approach (Australian stage and now Hollywood movie actor), taking part in some great stage plays like *Elizabeth*, *The Power of One* and *A Kid in King Arthur's Court*. He acted in a number of good first-rate films around making the Bond films with *Lara Croft: Tomb Raider*, *Road to Perdition*, *Sword of Honour*, *Munich*, *The Golden Compass* and *Cowboys and Aliens*. Craig made a guest appearance as *James Bond 007* at the opening ceremony of the *London 2012 Olympic Games*.

Like Brosnan and Dalton before him, Craig's attempt at Bond was met with scepticism and dissatisfaction from critics, stating it would not work and that Bond had had his day. But *Casino Royale* became the highest grossing Bond film at the box office, and the most recent Bond film, *Skyfall*, going past *Casino Royale* to be the most successful. Whatever one may think of Craig and the portrayal of Bond in the new era, Craig has definitely quietened the critics to become one of the most successful Bonds (Bio-graphy, 'Daniel Craig Biography'/ Personal Experiences – Watched James Bond 007 movies; / Personal Experiences- University).

## Movie Makers

### Ian Fleming and Albert R. Broccoli and Harry Saltzman

Author of the *James Bond 007* novels, *Ian Fleming*, and co-producers of the Bond films, *Albert R. Broccoli and Harry Saltzman*, were geniuses in their own right. There were other movies and television shows dedicated to detective and secret agent work, like *The Saint* with Roger Moore and *Remington Steele* for Pierce Brosnan, but none compared to *James Bond 007*. Fleming, together with Broccoli and Saltzman, brought Bond to life. According to Wikipedia and 'James Bond in film' profile, film companies initially rejected Broccoli and Saltzman, calling them " 'too British' " and " 'too blatantly sexual' " and funny enough this came through in the films.

The British side of Bond was not really explored in most, if not all of the films, for example, breakfast teas and bangas (sausages) and mash and Football. The only moments when something British came up in Bond was when shots of Britain were shown whilst Bond was making his way to or was at MI6 headquarters and Bond was shown briefly speaking to those at the headquarters, i.e. Miss Moneypenny, Q for the gadgets and the head of MI6, who all had some British accent. Of course all the actors who played Bond were from Great Britain (Bio-graphy, 'Ian Fleming Biography'/ Bio-graphy, 'Albert R. Broccoli and Harry Saltzman Biography'/ Personal Experiences – Watched James Bond 007 movies/ Personal Experiences- University).

Still, little of the British way of life and culture was looked at or depicted. However, was this really necessary when the real aim was to show Bond as a secret agent. However, American film companies should acknowledge the contribution of Britain to the world.

*Ian Fleming's* novels were a fantastic contribution to literature but also potentially to movie making. Labelling Broccoli and Saltzman as 'too blatantly sexual' came through in the Bond films with Bond's charm, suave, flirting and sexual energy and contact with the Bond girls, and in a light way with Miss Moneypenny. The general population of Lazenby, Connery and Moore's era were probably not used to all of this sexual connotations, being a bit more naive. At least Bond showed some good intention and approach with these women instead of just jumping all over them or going straight to bed with them. This was shown to be a part of Bond, almost like 'love-on-the-run' (Bio-graphy, 'Ian Fleming Biography'/ Bio-graphy, 'Albert R. Broccoli and Harry Saltzman Biography'/ Personal Experiences – Watched James Bond 007 movies/ Personal Experiences- University).

On the 21st of October, 1954, *CBS* paid *Ian Fleming* $1,000 to adapt his book Casino Royale into a one-hour television adaptation. A thousand dollars does not seem that much today, but was a lot back then, and it was a start for Fleming who managed to get onto CBS, a big television company then and now. One hour did not do justice to Fleming's *Casino Royale*, missing important parts of the book, but still retaining the action and violence.

Of course the action was rated as more important, but it came at the cost of other significant elements such as themes and dialogue. Surely, Fleming could have helped this one hour adaptation to take place, but possibly *CBS* movie makers may have been pushy. This was the only time an American-actor, Barry Nolan, played the part of Bond, otherwise Broccoli and Saltzman used actors from the UK, and funny enough, in the modern era, films in America were usually connected with action (Bio-graphy, 'Ian Fleming Biography'/ IanFleming.com/ Personal Experiences – Watched James Bond 007 movies/Personal Experiences - University).

Fleming wrote the Bond novels in Jamaica, the same place *Goldfinger* was filmed. Jamaica is a beautiful and tropical location that would have provided fantastic inspiration for Fleming. It is amazing how many Bond books Fleming came up with, showing his creativity and ingenuity. People can view the covers of the original books on *Google* or buy them from book companies like Amazon.com. It would be interesting to read a Bond book by Fleming, trying to imagine and picture what was going on in the novel.

Fiction and non-fiction novels have exploded in popularity with online book retailers, like *Amazon* and *ebay*, becoming very successful. With the Bond films, Fleming's books were never promoted alongside the films, which they originated from. Perhaps Fleming wanted to keep the books away from the films because it might ruin the imagery portrayed in them. Still, there would be a large number of people who would have, and still can have a read of Fleming's books (Bio-graphy, 'Ian Fleming Biography'/ IanFleming.com/ Personal Experiences – Watched James Bond 007 movies/ Personal Experiences- University).

It would be interesting to see how Fleming contributed to the Bond films. Fleming knew Bond more than anyone else because he created the character. Fleming would have passed on some good advice and knowledge about Bond's style and charm and how and what he said, for example, lines like 'Martini, shaken not stirred' and 'Bond, James Bond', amongst other things. It is not known whether Broccoli and Saltzman actually utilised Fleming's expertise in future Bond films.

Once the stage was set with the initial or first James Bond film, surely Fleming's knowledge and skill would have followed into the other Bond films. Perhaps Fleming's advice, knowledge and skill was kept on file to refer to for later Bond films. Then again, there are also Fleming's novels to refer to as something may have been missed or ignored (Bio-graphy, 'Ian Fleming Biography'/ IanFleming.com/ Personal Experiences – Watched James Bond 007 movies/Personal Experiences- University).

**The Audience**

A search on Google found few results for specific audiences of James Bond. However, the MI6 Community and Yahoo! Answers provided some simple, straightforward and direct facts and information for the general target audience of the Bond films. Bond fans definitely like one thing, and that is action. Bond has plenty of action in it to satisfy a hardened action fan. When a viewer thinks action, somewhere in there would be *James Bond 007*. The thing is, there are so many other things in Bond films to keep things going, enjoyable and entertaining. There are fans who like the early cinematography of Bond in all its glory, and this would include film and drama students. Then there are fans who like the style and charm and dialogue of the James Bond character or the actors who play Bond, the music, the Bond girls and love scenes, technology, the job of a secret agent, the battle of good and bad, and so on (MI6 Community, March 18-24/Yahoo! Answers, 'Who is the Target Audience for James Bond films?' / Personal Experiences – Watched James Bond 007 movies/ Personal Experiences- University).

The demographics of Bond fans would mainly include Baby Boomers, with regards to the older Bond era of Lazenby, Connery and Moore. Baby Boomers grew up on films when film first came out to the general public and were around when the initial Bond films were made and shown to the public, including the introduction of colour to films. Film companies have even brought out a complete collection of Bond films from the old and new eras for fans of today and Bond films frequent free-to-air and cable television channels from time-to-time.

These fans grew up on George Lanzby, Sean Connery and Roger Moore. With the new era of Bond, younger generations were exposed to Bond, but with new characters like Timothy Dalton, Pierce Brosnan and Daniel Craig. This exposure to younger generations would have influenced them to explore, research and reminisce on older Bond films and their characters (MI6 Community, March 18-24/Yahoo! Answers, 'Who is the Target Audience for James Bond films?' / Personal Experiences – Watched James Bond 007 movies/ Personal Experiences- University).

It would have been interesting to see these fans' comparison of older and younger Bond films. Whether it is Baby Boomers or the younger generation, these fans were moviegoers. They may enjoy classical or epic films, similar to Roman or religious films like *Ben-Hur* and *Moses*, or those on *Turner Classic Movies (TCM)* on cable television. Such fans are mainly low-middle to middle and upper class residents and citizens and like the better things in life, or quality, and possible extravagance, have a reasonable or solid income and value safety and security. Some of these fans could actually be from defence, security and emergency crews who live life on the edge, help people in need like Bond and battle bad people for a living (MI6 Community, March 18-24/Yahoo! Answers, 'Who is the Target Audience for

James Bond films?' / Personal Experiences – Watched James Bond 007 movies/ Personal Experiences- University).

Most films these days cater for the younger generation, particularly young males 16 to 30 years of age, and Bond in the modern era has been changed somewhat to accompany this group. Younger viewers want to see it all, and Bond old and new, softer and harder respectively, caters to this to a large degree. From violence and weapons to love and secret agents. Bond is a film that can fit all these areas, which is the reason why it is still so popular today. Some movie makers should be calling on the views, creativity, skill and expertise of the public, old and new, to provide some new directions and angles, including producing and directing. Some scripts and footage can be sent in to see what people can come up with. An example is finding more *Ian Fleming*-like novelists, as mentioned earlier, movie makers or contributors who can think and create something for the Bond films (MI6 Community, March 18-24/Yahoo! Answers, 'Who is the Target Audience for James Bond films?' / Personal Experiences – Watched James Bond 007 movies/ Personal Experiences- University).

### 3. Conclusion

There are probably better actors to play *James Bond 007*, who have it all and do it all. Sean Connery was, and Daniel Craig is, of a high standard of Bond, but the way young people are these days there are Bond-potentials who are crazier than those of old, yet can still maintain all that is Bond. Movie makers have got to start thinking which direction Bond and the series of Bond films will take. Viewers, including Bond fans, are getting tired of the same thing, especially all the action and a supposed, or apparent, lack of charm, dialogue, storyline and 'oomph'. It would be crazy to change the tried-and-true lines of Bond, like 'Martini, shaken not stirred', so something else needs to be done. Perhaps another weird and wonderful theme or angle, such as time-travel, James Bond in pre-historic times, some type of car racing like Formula One or Bond in the media. Surely there would be numerous directions to possibly take for Bond. In the process, whilst some viewers and fans may be lost, others can be gained. A big resource is getting back the Baby Boomers who were in love with the old Bond actors of George Lazenby, Sean Connery and Roger Moore.

# 4. Bibliography

- 007James (www.007James.com/characters) 'James Bond Characters'

  - Auric Goldfinger
  - Dr. No
  - James Bond 007
  - List of All James Bond Girls
  - Top 10 James Bond Villians
  - Jaws
  - M
  - Miss Moneypenny
  - Red Grant
  - Q

- Bio (Bio-graphy.com):

  - Albert R. Broccoli and Harry Saltzman Biography
  - Daniel Craig Biography
  - Ian Fleming Biography
  - Sean Connery Biography
  - Pierce Brosnan Biography
  - Roger Moore Biography

- Bond Lifestyle – www.jamesbondlifestyle.com
- Box Office Mojo, 'James Bond 007', IMDb

- Los Angeles Times (November 10, 2012) 'James Bond: Four writers carry forward Ian Fleming's spy legacy'.

- MI6 Community (March 18-24)

- Personal Experiences:

  – Watched most of James Bond 007 movies with family and friends, on free-to-air and cable television, particularly the

Sean Connery-Roger Moore era, and have the James Bond 007 movie collection.

- Watched various action films on free-to-air and cable television and Internet, for example, films of Arnold Schwarzenegger, Sylvestor Stallone, Bruce Willis, The Bourne Ultimatum and Austin Powers
- University: Learned to write properly from tutors and lecturers and student centre at University.

- Yahoo! Answers, 'Who is the Target Audience for James Bond films?'